Total Depravity

Total Depravity
Poems

H. C. Kim

The Hermit Kingdom Press
Cheltenham   Seoul   Bangalore   Cebu City

Total Depravity: Poems

All Rights Reserved © 2004 by H. C. Kim

No part of this book may be reproduced or transmitted in any form or by any means, graphic, electronic, or mechanical, including photocopying, recording, taping, or by any information storage retrieval system, without the permission in writing from the publisher.

For information address:

The Hermit Kingdom Press
Suite 291
48 Regent Street
Cambridge
CB2 1FD
United Kingdom

info@TheHermitKingdomPress.com

http://www.TheHermitKingdomPress.com

ISBN: 0-972-38643-2

Dedicated to All Who Inspire

"There is no one righteous, not even one."

Romans 3:10
THE HOLY BIBLE

Contents

Preface 13

"The Muse of Tossa de Mar" 15

"The Monologue" 16

"The Printer on the Table" 17

"Radio Static" 20

"The Computer Screen" 22

"USB Cord" 24

"Yet, I Don't" 25

"Cracked Glasses" 27

"A Fence High and Mighty" 28

"Drizzle" 29

"Sun Is Out" 31

"Two Mermaids" 32

"The Sun Strikes" 33

"Lingerie Shop" 35

"Sun Pressing Down" 37

"Autumn Sunshine" 39

"Tree Touched by Rain" 42

"Small Chili Peppers" 43

Contents

"A Soccer Shirt"...46

"Basketball Match"..48

"Compsci"..50

"Exam in Full Swing"..52

"Exam Outfits"..54

"Exam Periods"...56

"Flat"...58

"Library"...59

"Movement"...60

"Queens' English"...61

"Single Diversion"...62

"Sky Blue"..63

"The Passage of Time"...64

"The Water Bottle Girl"...66

"Thoughts in the Library"..68

"Through the Window"...70

"Typing Away"...72

"Under a Tree"..75

"Her Bottle Of Liquid"...76

"Images"...77

Contents

"Base Passions" 78

"Deterrence" 80

"Drawn" 83

"I Met Her" 85

"Passing By" 87

"Purple" 89

"She Raises Her Finger" 95

"The Smile" 97

"The Way She Moved" 98

"Dampened Lawn" 100

"Grass and White Flowers" 102

"Motionless" 104

"The Glacier" 105

"The Oasis" 107

"Beyond" 110

"Click, Slip, Flip" 111

"Through the Garden" 112

"The Sun Rises" 114

Preface

What makes us human, but the experience of the good and the bad, both outside of us and inside of us? This collection of poems brings together expressions of participation in the human experience.

H. C. Kim
Valentine's Day 2004
Jesus College
Cambridge

"THE MUSE OF TOSSA DE MAR"

Glistening in the sun
Like the Sahara Desert
Gently undulating hills of golden sand
Finely textured

Shining under the radiance
Warm and intense
Sunshine reaching its peak
In the middle of the day

There she lay
On the sandy beach of Tossa de Mar
Her skin bronzed by the touch of the sun
Her body becoming one with the surrounding sand

Music still playing in her ears
As the Muse of the sea
Sang
Caught between two rocky mountains

The rough with the gentle
Contrasts commingling in harmony
As the din of sun worshippers rose
Sea breeze bouncing off of their bodies

Her body curving in practical precision
Directed by her feminine being
As if sending out an invitation
A welcome for a man's touch

There she lay purposefully
With every inch of her in perfect agreement
Like a chorus beautifully sung
I heard her music

"THE MONOLOGUE"

My fingers rolled off her body
Like a snowball slowly rolling down the hill
With each advance
Greater mass was gained

As her body responded
By bouncing my fingers playfully
In an unintentional sanction
Tingling with each gentle pressure

Energy mass gathering in her body's core
Transferring heat to my being through the contact
Blood pumping in synchronicity
Matching the boiling sun's intensity

Like pushing snowball up the hill
To plant the entity on top
Snowman smiling
With a twinkle in his eyes

My fingers push up against her elevation
Collecting her essential mass
Bringing a spark to her eyes
Shining underneath the sun's warmth

Her soft skin moves underneath my hand
In a patterned vibration
Complementing her soft
Yet audible breathing

She lay there without a word
Seemingly passive
Yet her body spoke out loud
In a clear, intentioned monologue

"THE PRINTER ON THE TABLE"

My white printer on the table
Lies demure on a wooden board
Her fine form completely symmetric
Facing me

Her curves gently flow
Visually enticing
Form
Smooth body

Her white body shining under the room light
Magnificently protruding in her nakedness
She lies there in her firm frame
Ready to receive

I gently feed my paper
Pressing against her back
Feeding her piece by piece
As paper glides smoothly in

Slot made for reception
A part of her fine being
I hold my paper there for a while
Before letting go

Her front tray is extended
Spread out before me
Attached to her front
Her center orifice

I can see the intricate details of her opening
Made for producing new creation
Intelligence imprinted on her output
Making her offspring a part of her

It is this beautiful opening of creation
That rests open on top of the wooden board

Total Depravity

Almost as if staring at me
As if it had eyes

As wet ink flows
Inside her wide-open entrance
Buzzing her being
The wooden board underneath her shaking in excitement

My paper goes into her
Deeper and deeper
As her finely oiled machinery turns and turns
In her constant lubricated state

I do it again
As she certainly requires more paper
I feed my paper into her back
Pressing gently

She buzzes
Her frame shaking
Sound filling the room
As paper goes deeper and deeper in

I turn my attention to her front opening
The intricate entry point
Delicate in her make up
Capable of doing so much

It feels like my paper is stuck
My paper is jammed tightly against her opening
Crumpled in pressure
I push and pull

Push
Pull
Press
Press

I feel my paper stuck in her being
I can feel the wetness of her ink
On my page
And I gently pull my paper free

Total Depravity

She's rolling again
Her frame shakes
Generating a lot of musical sounds
And I can see my paper coming out of her orifice

Slowly
It pulls out
As the wooden board squeaks
Underneath the presser

Again
My paper is stuck
Tightly in her opening
Her lips tightly holding onto my page

I firmly push
Pressing my paper into her
Before gently pulling out
I do it again

Pushing in
Pushing out
This time a little bit more firmly
With a bit of pressure inserted

The paper comes out
I hold my page firmly in my hands
And appreciate the opening from which it came
Her wet ink imprinted now drying

My white printer lies there
In its firm profundity
Oh, the things she can do
And the pleasure she brings to my life

She lies there
Fulfilled
In her glory
My beautiful partner in creation

"RADIO STATIC"

Static pervades the room
Shrill sounds cutting through the air
Like a broken carburetor egging away

I look at the book in front of me
And remember the last scene
The picturesque, visual scene of the story

The happy ending the storyline promised
The beauty of the main character
As if I could look into her eyes and read her heart

Radio static breaks the memory into pieces
Like the broken vessel in Kabala
Picturing the whole world disrupted and broken

Violently the radio static invades
Like a poisonous germ cell created in a test tube
By Mr. Hyde

Yet, I remember
The gentleness of the words
Smooth flow of long, long paragraphs

Serenity of the scenes
The presence of something very special
Like a pretty seashell lying on a sunbathed white beach

With blue, blue skies endless
Soft clouds plucking away at the bright blue
Excited waves stroking one another

I long to pick up the book
To devour each and every page
To drink with my eyes the beauty within

Total Depravity

To see where next pages will lead
What exciting developments await
Joys and sorrows to be shared together

The images linger in my mind's eye
As I remain
Stopped by the persistent radio static

"THE COMPUTER SCREEN"

The computer screen stares back at me
As if seeking understanding
Watching to comprehend
To see what I am thinking

As I caress her body
Pressing her buttons
Rolling my fingers over her protrusions
Pressing firmly to get the result

Her keys letting out sounds
Passively relenting
But with constant buzzing
Sounds come flowing

I gaze back at her blank stare
Interrupted by words that seem to pop out
Imprinting her blankness
With deep meaning

Like well-moisturized crystallite
In a damp, dark, hidden cave
Radiating at a ray of flashlight
The screen lets out luminescence

I touch her body
With my eager fingers
Wanting more
To see more

I feel the stoic gaze of her blank screen
A façade
Heat raging underneath
Electricity traveling at the speed of light

Total Depravity

I can feel the hum of her body
The buzz of her being
I can feel the noise of her generator
And the life source of her essence

I type away
Imprinting my digits
Into her
Forcing my fingers gently into her body

The computer screen stares back
Not taking her eyes off of me
I can't quite tell if she approves
As I have my way with her keyboard

She remains receiving
And I can't help but to continue
To fill her screen
With words I impute into her being

"USB CORD"

The USB cord is coiled
Twisting in an egg shaped loop
The line curving upwards
In a firm spiral

Its long, over-extended length
Making its way around
Curving
Wrapping

Gently on the desk
Lying there satiated
After an electronic exhaustion
Having performed its maximum

But ready
Willing to go at it again
To generate energy
To produce information

Waiting to be linked
To be plugged in
To the empty socket
Computer heating after being pressed on

Connection to be made
Becoming one in being
Moving information together
Co-mingling in cyber-connection

The USB cord is wrapped on itself
Its arm resting gently on its body
Waiting
To be inter-linked

"YET, I DON'T"

I see
Yet, I don't

Like a rare white flower
On the hills of English countryside
Caught in a glimpse
While driving quickly by

Backing up
It's gone
Like the puff of a magic dragon
That exists in imagination

I feel
Yet, I don't

Like the breath of cool air
Emanating through the open window
Of an air-conditioned office
Where a finely gloomed secretary sits

A brief hug of coolness
In the sweltering heat of the summer
A fleeting moment in a long walk
Heat forces to forget the cool feel

I taste
Yet, I don't

Like the juicy apple
Just plucked from the apple tree
In the apple orchard
In Pennsylvania

Natural waters
Dripping down one's tongue
In the memory
Of years past

Total Depravity

I know
Yet, I don't

Her love
Those searching eyes
Her nervousness
Betraying her trained composure

Is it something that I saw?
Or did I just imagine?
Wishful thinking
Of my own love-stricken heart?

Total Depravity

"CRACKED GLASSES"

Fumbling across the road
A clear path
Appearing cloudy and tricky
Viewing through broken glasses

Sunshine entered in prism
In broken rays
Sprayed in all directions
Beauty shattered

A pretty world awaits
In the short distance
Full of wonder
Filled with joy

But alas
Broken view
Slows down the progress
Bumbling along

It stretches and stretches
Like a path over mountains
Across a desiccated dessert
Through high seas

It is only at an arm's length
Love fulfilled
And the accompanying joy
But cracked glasses hinder like a broken heart

"A FENCE HIGH AND MIGHTY"

A fence high and mighty
Atop a stone wall
History-bound
A bastion of learning and knowledge

Interrupted only by tree branches
Wooden
Fragile
Naked

How they entangle themselves
In a web of most unwholesome intrigue
Choking the life out of the regal fence
Apparently vulnerable

Life flowing through the thin branches
Jutting upwards
Sideways
Throughout the fence

Caught in the enmeshed chaos
Reality commingled with fiction
Feelings enthralled by duty
Social obligations and personal desire

The austere fence keeps them out
Or is it in?
But going nowhere
The two seem interlocked in a stalemate

In a game neither can win
Future hindered by the present
The entryway blocked
By some unexplainable law of nature

"DRIZZLE"

Drizzle
Drops of rain water
Falling
Hitting the floor
Making audible sounds

Like the sound of bath water down the drain
Soft tap of hands on naked flesh
Quick flapping of bed sheets
Running finger nails gently on a flat surface
Roller coaster slowly rolling down a curved path

Reminiscent of morning shower
Squirts of water in a swimming pool frolic
Water gushing forth to put out a raging flame
Flower treated with drops of life producing liquid
Sprinklers going off on grass

Smell fresh
Like walking into a sanitized hospital room
Feeling the newness of just washed pajamas
Hot steamed towel pressed against one's nose
Tongue touching just manicured finger nails

Everything is soaked
Head uncovered underneath the heavenly effusion
Arms bare without protection
The shirt that covers the body
As well as the skin-binding pants

Hair stringy from its wetness
Face glowing in its shiny coating
Lips shining as if whetted by special spices
Eyes glistening like sparkling wine bathing in sunshine
Drops of water running down the long neck slowly

Total Depravity

Drizzle
Water bangs the pavement
Sound resonating throughout the neighborhood
Like that of one in intense happiness
Music to those who feel

"SUN IS OUT"

Sun is shining again
It was horribly overcast yesterday
Drizzling rain
Dark murkiness
Simply unpleasant

Today
Sun is shining
High over the heavens
Penetrating the expanding skies
Glorious scenery

Library is becoming emptier
People are done with exams
Some in the full swing of celebration
Others are taking their last exams
Before diving into summer

Few people still plug away
Those unfortunate enough to have exams
Extending into the final weeks
Research students
Who are in it for the long haul

The sun is brightly shining
For all those who would enjoy it
Partake of its nature fellowship
Even partially in passing
It is a glorious day

"TWO MERMAIDS"

There they were!
Out of the water
Beautiful sea creatures
Golden hair glistening in the sun

Enticing in its wetness
Drenched in salty waters
Freshly out of the water
Drops of water flowing down their shoulders

Strands of hair sticking to their long necks
Beautiful in their ethereal transcendence
Milky white, shining in the sun
Smooth and without blemish

Two mermaids adorning the pages of fairy tales
Right there on earth
In flesh and blood
With glowing smiles that belie their material reality

They sit there
With their beautiful long legs outstretched
Shining in sun-stroked beach
Fine sand sticking to their beautiful form

Unaware
They smile
And the sounds of the sea
The din of summer frolic recedes in the background

The two testimonies to feminine beauty shine in their glory
Like angels descended from heaven to earth
With beauty not for the faint of heart
But with heavenly innocence

How did the two beautiful sea creatures wash up ashore?
It seems that the space of this sand is unworthy before their feet
As they speak in soft, sweet tones
A part of their glorious presence

"THE SUN STRIKES"

The sun is beating down
Mercilessly
Casting heavy blows
Pushing and shoving
Striking

Like a merciless master
Cracking a whip on a slave's shoulder
The sun lashes
Heat stroke after heat stroke
Sweat runs like blood gushing from opened skin

The sun glares in anger
Ready to pounce on the helpless
Drawing a deathblow
Upon a populace unready
Its angry face too intense to gaze upon

As a strong warrior
Who has never seen defeat
Or knows pity
The sun waves its death sword of fire
Seeing to the demise of thousands

People run and hide
From the fiery wrath of the sun
Rushing towards the shade
Where they would not be seen
In the cool recess of a hideout

Some rush and plunge
Deep into the ocean bottom
Feeling that they can find solace there
Protection from the elements
Welcome among sea creatures

Total Depravity

But most have no choice but to remain
Hoping for mercy from the heartless striker
Suffocating as the sun casually
Wraps its swift hands around the throat
With its burning passion

Hope does not seem to exist
As one, two, three drop dead
Victims of sun's unforgiving wrath
Four, five, six
Many more dead

The sun strikes
With crazed frenzy
Putting fear in the hearts of all
Weak and strong alike
For who knows who will be struck next?

"LiNGERiE SHOP"

I sit here, waiting
In front of the lingerie shop
Don't ask me how I came to sit here
I just found an open table

But I find myself directly looking into a shop before me
It's a woman's underwear shop
Transparent bras and panties
Literally highlighted by mannequins with bright lights inside

They are transparent
And it makes me a bit embarrassed to look at them
Yes, they are dummies with light bulbs
But it's the suggestion of the clothing that reddens

Now, I understand why people threw me the glance
That stare
No, honest
I did not sit here on purpose

It is interesting that there is a lingerie shop
Here in the airport
I wonder how much business they get
It is interesting clothing on dislplay

Who knew such things existed
Most men live a life-time without
Throwing a glance into a women's lingerie shop
A lot of different, bold styles

Some older women walk in
Perhaps to surprise their husbands
Or maybe they have a lover on the side?
This is Europe after all

I sit here in bewilderment
Thinking that the stares are passing ones

Total Depravity

It's not like I am being observed at length
It's not like a reality show

A mom walks in with her little son
Another mom joins in
You know where their husbands are
They would not be caught dead in such a shop

The façade of the shop is completely open
Like the other front-wall-less shops next to it
A book shop to the right
An electronics shop to the left

Wait a minute!
A guy walked out of the shop
Wonder if he is interested in a purchase for himself
He's the only guy in the last 30 minutes

They call panties
Knickers here in England
Just a small fact
Wonder what the history of that word is

I sit here
As I wait for my flight
People pass by and stare
I don't care any more

"SUN PRESSING DOWN"

The sun is pressing down on me
Like gentle hands slowly pushing
I can feel the warmth of the heat rise
And I revel in the sweet experience

Not unlike gentle wind stroking my body
The sunshine spreads over my body
I can only long for more
As I experience a natural high

As my back presses against the naked grass
Green marks left on my bare legs
Shorts smudged in earth colors
I spread my hands wide against the short stubbles

Drops of sweat gathers
They even feel like burning up
From my body heat
Fueled by the energy of the sun

I want to turn over
To allow my other side
To exude in the heavenly touch
Heated stroke

But I find myself almost helpless
So relaxed
In near ecstatic state
Would the sun flip me over!

Turned over
My stomach presses against
The stomach of the earth
I can almost hear the heartbeat of the earth's core

My cheek is tickled by the grass
With the sweet aroma of recently received rain showers

Total Depravity

My lips near the lips of the wild grass
I desire to partake

To be a part of the earth's sweet embrace
To touch the beauty of nature with my body
To receive sunshine's radiant glance
To engage in a mystic intercourse

I could feel the coolness of my stomach
As my back burns with heat
Sunshine caressing my back
From bottom to top

I lie there
Wanting more
Desiring to be taken
By the sun's ways

"AUTUMN SUNSHINE"

Autumn sunshine drifts in
And sets itself on the seat of nature
Next to the gentle breeze
And the revealing legs of summer warmth

Summer warmth crosses
Over to entice the newcomer
Gentle gale lays open
To receive the hand of autumn sun rays

With pleasure
The sunshine caresses
Imprinting gently
Adding heat to zephyr

Willingly
Gentle breeze receives
Breathes pleasure
Frolicking laughter

Summer warmth indulges in her pleasure
Empathetically
Remembering the heat of summer sun
Ecstatic screams of youth by flowing waters

Warmth rises all over
Threesome of sensual expression
Busty bosom of summer
Autumn sun's passionate hand on the thigh of the impressive gale

Summer's remnant sensuality brought to self-expression
Coyly the summer breeze allows the newcomer
To pet her curvaceous movement
To linger by her sensitive area

Like a personal pleasure slave
Eagerly autumn sunshine obliges

Total Depravity

Adding slight pressure to induce climax
Fingers working their magic

The remnant summer engages the breeze
Carried over from the summer
Wanting to join in the fun
Surreptitious glance of desire

The newly arrived sun rays
Press against the side of summer breeze
Feeling the warmth of its bosom
Realizing the increase in mixture of want and guilt

Cold breeze exerts itself
Hand pushing away the hand of autumn sunshine
In frolic fun
With nervous coldness betraying her desire

Thorough intercourse
Of the sexy summer
Feminine gale
Eager but shy autumn sunshine just around the corner

A single boldness will bring about an explosion of ecstasy
Desires fully satisfied
Creativity pushed to the limit
Beyond wildest fantasies

Seconds away from the exchange of elements and fluids
Vapors carried by the autumn breeze
Squeezed between the well-known summer
And the new autumn sunshine

Sandwiched in between like
White slices of bread
A single slice of bologna
A lot of liquid sauce in between

Co-mingling
Interlocked in aesthetic twist
Mixture of fire and water

Total Depravity

Summer and fall

Autumn sunshine licking the gentle breeze
Being kissed by the remnant summer
Squeezed in all the right places
Desire rising on all sides

Light breeze bending
Copulating in the autumn sun
The tongue of remaining summer
Quickly making its way all over

Back and forth
Inside and out
Up and down
Against the wall

The gentle wind is pressed
Sunshine presses
The remnant summer encompasses
The pleasure of seasonal change

"TREE TOUCHED BY RAIN"

The tree once so dry and colorless
Comes alive
With a magical touch
Of the sporadic rainfall

Green color becomes vibrant
Like the bright face of a girl in front of a cherry lollypop
A birthday boy unraveling his favorite item
A woman looking down at the baby who came out of her body

Tree trunks are coated with shininess
Like brand new stockings on beautiful legs
A mean, lean driving machine just out of the production line
A silk slip that has not yet touched naked body

Leaves retain water
As if the wetness sprang out from within
Drops of liquid hang from their edges
As if teasing to be plucked

Rain drops fall from the leaves
Like pouring sweat of one who has just gone the mile
Squeezed sponge releasing soapy matter
Tea falling from a tightly squeezed plastic bottle

Water gathers by the tree trunk
Like naked toes on a sandy beach submerged in the incoming tide
Soapy fluid within the sink made by both hands
Lips touching the surface of a round pond

A stream of water effortlessly flows down the length of the tree
Like the crawl of a turtle up a gentle slope
Expert hands massaging down a soft back
Releasing tension and relieving pressure

"SMALL CHILI PEPPERS"

It is a bouquet
As beautiful as a dozen roses
With green stem
And red faces gently holding up on top

Like a grouping of roses
Color of passion sparks
As eyes behold
The redness of its fruit

Sumptuous to the eyes
Inviting a touch
Sexy in form
Red hot, small chili peppers

Unlike a gathering of roses
They can be tasted
Consumed
Devoured

Adding taste to anything
They touch
Heat of skin
Certainly will rise

Heart beating
Faster and faster
With the sensation
Sensitive and delicate

Small chili peppers
Surely could fit inside the mouth
Of a hot-blooded maiden
With bright red lipsticks

Total Depravity

They would be too hot to handle
Perhaps
Blood would boil
And the body would feel like it's on fire

Better take in small doses
Absorbing the taste
Gradually
Slowly

Enjoying small doses
Adding to a fixation
All of them will be inside
Deeply

Condiment
Adding spice to life
Zest to reality
Salivation

How could such a small thing
Bring so much
Pleasure?
Tasty

Not only beautiful to behold
Soliciting desire to touch
How I want to eat it!
Again and again

Until too much of a good thing
Would be just too much
A cry, "Can't have any more!"
Resounds from pleasured buds

Conjoined with the cry
"Yes! Yes!"
Wanting more
A paradox in nature

Total Depravity

The beautiful bouquet
Firmly grasped in small feminine hands
With small peppers dangling
Inviting and firm

"A SOCCER SHIRT"

It is a soccer shirt
Bright and yellow
Displaying the glory
Of the stars of a proud nation

Clinging tightly
To the naked human form
Smooth texture of polyester
Next to the smooth surface of a curvaceous body

A fan of soccer
A supporter of the team
Proud of the nation
Or just loving the feel of the touch

Shirt pressing against her heart
Filled with beauty
Like the stars in the sky
In a clear, warm summer night

How I would like to draw
Stars of the sky
On the shirt
Where the heart is

Like the passion of the sport
The emotions of the heart
Behind the shirt
Cannot be hidden

Should not be hidden
Although what is behind the shirt
Cannot be seen
What is there is there

Total Depravity

Emotions
Sensations
Hopes
And dreams

The tight soccer shirt
Bright in its florescent yellow
Sticking to the body form in every way
Gives a glimpse of all that could be

"BASKETBALL MATCH"

Bouncing of the orange ball
Against hard, rigid surface
Defense against offense
One set against the other

The ring in disarray
The basketball court-stand movable
Moved
Moving

Ball bouncing all the while
Two players
Set in friendly competition
Having a bit of fun

Conversation turns to the game of love
Should love be a game, I ask?
It ends up being, whether we like it or not
Conversation of love mixed in with tips regarding the basketball game

Effective defense is fast
Tries to put the opponent in a weaker position
Maximizes the strength of self
Minimizes the strength of the other

When is one fouled?
Set by the rules of the game
Sometimes varying from country to country
But the general rule is not to run into one who is stationary

Ball is bouncing
Below the sunny skies
Friendly competition
Engaging the rules of the game

Total Depravity

Ball is in the air
Vying for the hole in the sky
To go through
Rather than to bounce away

Sometimes the ball goes in
Other times the basket is totally missed
Sometimes the ball goes round and round in a circle
Before going into the hole

The ball is bouncing
As the conversation picks up
Inspired by the spirit of the game
And challenges that lie ahead

The ball floats in the air
In a smooth trajectory
Flying below the vast skies
Without touching the ring, it goes in

"COMPSCI"

Compsci
Chomsky
Kandinsky

Surreal
Analytical
Superficial

World-changing
Globe-encompassing
Life-enriching

Science
Cognitive Science
Linguistics

Philosophy
Art
Creativity

Window
Open
Door

Beginning
End
Middle

Restart
Regeneration
Renewal

Completion
Success
Beginning of the path

Total Depravity

Condenski
Chompski
Compsci

"EXAM IN FULL SWING"

It's the middle of the exam period
All is quiet on the western front
Not a friendly chatter
Laughter of youthful frolic

Just silence
Overpervading silence
The library is empty
Even student cafes are void

There is tension in the air
Signs reading: "Slience"
Splattered around the building
Invigilators in robes

This is it
And they know it
Exam is where you are substantiated
A year's work boils down to this

Summer waits
With its fun and excitement
Passions and love's little kisses
But there is only tension in the air

It's the exam period
A time of self-abnegation
On this Monday morning
It is really quiet

There sits a girl in protected blue long-sleeve
Biting her pinky nail
Highlighting her law text
With a pearl earring contrasting her tanned French-like skin

Total Depravity

Next to her sits undoubtedly an English gal
With her fair skin and her single long braid
Resting on her shirt that reads:
"I love NY"
And she is chewing her nails

Next to her diagonally
Sits a girl with her back turned
Pink shirt that reads: "Show girls 2"
And she was biting her nails
But she is bent over her texts now

All three intensely engaged
Exam looming before
Trying to concentrate so hard
That thoughts must certainly scatter from the intensity

Intensity on their faces is not easy to behold
You see, they never look that intense
At least not in the library
Or in student cafes

Perhaps, if the opportunity presented itself
I might behold their beautifully intense
Faces in other contexts
That might not have the doom of exam in the background

Perhaps red roses carelessly thrown on the floor
With jazz music filling the air
To the subtle intensity of perfume on bare skin
Over the purple satin sheets

It is the exam period
All is quiet in here
In oppressive intensity
Of solitude of study

"EXAM OUTFITS"

They are all covered up, today
Like the clouds that won't let the sun
Shine gloriously
Exhibiting its magnificent rays

They have jackets zippered up to the top
Sweatshirts with hoods covering all of the neck
Long sleeve white shirts
It's like winter in here

It's spring
But who would know it?
With them closed
Closed in

It is exam time
Sleepless nights
Intense studying
When they feel unattractive

It is a psychological state of being
Fear mixed in with anticipation
Energy spent on books
No emotional energy left for anything else

Huddled over
One covering the space for three
Almost inconsiderately
Who can think of anything but this?

It's the exam time
A selfish period in the academic year
A time of renunciation and abnegation
Denial

Total Depravity

No
It is time for no's
Objections
An emotionally freezing time

A winter isolated in spring time
Frosty storm localized in fixed space
Snow blowing any warmth away
It is a time for exam outfits

"EXAM PERIODS"

Sitting here
Hearing a machine fall apart
God knows what it might mean
Pages turning
An artificial owl crying outside
You can feel the tension in the air
Collective anxiety
Broken only by ruffled papers

Exams ahead
One chance in a year to prove yourself
It ain't important what went before
All hangs on the exam
Pressure
Stress
What makes life worth living?
Even if it may not seem so now

Time flows
The sun rises and sets
It seems faster during exam time
Voices muffled
Silenced
All else in the background
Exam seems paramount
The only thing that matters

Foolishness!
Life goes on
With or without the exams
Life is not validated by these exams
Or negated
Can happiness be obtained through them?
Well, not really
No

Total Depravity

But the intensity goes on
Intensifying
It is the order of things
It's always been that way
Slaves to the institution
What went before dictating what goes on in the future
Without questioning their fundamental importance
The meaning of life

To be alive
To breathe
To know
To experience
How much more there is to life
Than what's contained between hard covers
Memories more precious than diamonds
Missed because of exam periods

"FLAT"

It's a flat kind of a day
The moistures seem to linger
Neither rain nor bright sunshine
Clouds covering the sky

Pretty visage of summer green
Trees aesthetically pleasing
With reddish leaves
Yellowish green ones as well

But it's still a flat kind of a day
Everything seems leveled
Like a vast plain
Like Holland

No mountains
Undulating hills
Passionate sunshine
Offensive rain

Everything vapid
Insipid
Dry
Flat

It's nearing the exam week
And things seem to go flat
Perhaps flatness will dissipate afterwards?
There will be more, just a little bit more?

Sun with greater intensity
Rain with more fiery noise
Mountains and round hills
Like the ones you see in the Alps

Life filled with greater zest
Hilly, rolling, undulating
Not boring
Certainly not flat

"LIBRARY"

Crisp turning of the page
Rip of the page breaking the calm
A flu inflicted student coughing
Who knows what germs she's spreading?
One sitting with a recent flu shot
A patch
A very small one
Taped to the upper left arm
Goings and comings
Sitting and standing
Reading and thinking
Whispering and shushing
Rustle of the passersby
Stroke of a highlighter pen
How loud it sounds!
In a library
On a sunny day
In a closed, suffocating space

"MOVEMENT"

Tilting her head
Her golden hair flowing down her shoulders
Like the gentle streams of Niagara's river
Her snowy, white hands pressed against her pen
Thoughts appear elsewhere
But seemingly working on her law project
I bet
The term's end is around the corner
The joyful occasion of Christmas a few weeks away
White Christmas
Red stockings
Blinking lights
Cozy fireplace
Spirit of joy
Promises of a new year
All drifting forward in time
Thoughts of past and present
She stands up
Greets a friend
Both, hand in hand
Head towards the snack stand
Standing around there
A break from the rigors
Into a reality altogether another
Or is it?
She stands waiting for her order
Her golden hair shining under the iridescent light
Just like out of a picture book
In a long black coat
Dark shirt tightly holding onto her body
I caught a glance as she quickly headed toward the snack stand
And here she is coming back
This way
She, her friend, and another friend added
In the bustle of the snack room
As I wait on a bench
My back pressed against the wall
Wondering what she is thinking
As she chews her sandwich

Total Depravity

"QUEENS' ENGLISH"

Chatting away
In a proper English accent
At least it sounds to me that way
Two first year students from Queens'

One is done with her exams
The other in an exam limbo
Both apparently without any care in the world
It's quite different from all that is around all over here

Chatting away about everything
About nothing
All the while it sounds beautiful
I can't but sit and listen to the melodious chatter

Two English blondes
Full of life
Energy
Imbued with the spirit of Queens' English

First year
I wonder what they have experienced
One confesses to gaining Queens' English
Here upon arrival

On my part
I could not but confess
I loved to hear them talk
And I wouldn't mind hearing them talk all night long

In Queens' English they chatted
With no care in the world
I was lost in their sexy accents
Not concerned about the content of what was said

Long live the Queen
And Queens' English
The beautiful bastion of English culture and power
And here's to the Church of England

"SINGLE DIVERSION"

Ruddy cheeks
Flushed red
As if having imbibed choicest wines
From fantastic, distant lands

Lips
Rosy
Vibrant with life
Complimenting her elated state

Arms
Colored
With pinkish, teasing freckles
In harmony

Smile
Playing in her face
Dancing in a subtle way
Enticing in its mystery

Eyes
Lowered
But with fiery energy
Piercing through to the soul

She remains
There sitting
In the midst of her friends
As the single diversion

"SKY BLUE"

Sky blue shines through a silky screen
Whiteness of being
Overtaken by the vastness of the reaching
Color of promises
Of infinity

Like wilderness
Covered over by running animals
In the safari fields
Kicking up dust
Pushing up commotion

Clipped underneath the veil
Blueness of possible expression
Awaiting expression
Appreciation
Devouring

What can one clad in orange do?
But think of the combination
Orange with blue
Veiled together under the silk screen
Smoothly rubbing against one another

"THE PASSAGE OF TIME"

It is the passage of time
Like the flowing of the melting snow
Atop a glossy glacier
Imperceptible
Yet a certain attrition
Fundamentally shifting reality
What makes what
What it is

That captures our imagination
Imprisons our person
Binds our ties
Limits our potential
Stifles the imaginative possibilities
Leaving one
Helpless
Weak

Time lost
Beauty fleeting
Friendships withering away
Flesh moving closer and closer to earth
But memories do remain
Pictures are added to the photo albums
Little address book no longer with space
The end of the world seems closer

But the flow of time
Is also like salmon flowing upstream
Fighting the currents
Finding meaning in the struggle
With desire to procreate
To create
To propagate
To expand

Total Depravity

And even more is the beauty of time
And the aggregate passions
More pronounced
In the presence of a beautiful woman
With clear blue eyes
Flowing hair gently resting on her bare neck
Writing away whatever she is
Unaware of the desire she raises

"THE WATER BOTTLE GIRL"

I saw the water bottle girl today
With her typical posse of followers
Standing in line
To pick up another water bottle

You see
Her water bottle was empty
And it needed a refilling
But it looks like she wanted to replace the whole thing

She stood there in the line
Firmly grasping her empty bottle
With one hand
Not wanting to let go

Her two friends
Standing around her
Bottleless
Obviously admiring her

And she talked confidently
Even I could see that
And she advanced
Towards the front

Another water bottle, please
I imagined her to say
But she's too classy to say that
What would she say?

She will have her water bottle
All filled up with another load
To be unloaded in her mouth
It should last her for a while at least

Total Depravity

I wonder how many water bottles
Her small self would go through
In a typical term period
She seems always walking around with it

Now she comes
With a smile on her face
Her full water bottle in her hand
I don't see the empty one anymore

Did she chuck it?
Throw it in the bin like yesterday's newspaper?
I look
Just because I am curious

She opens the water bottle and drinks
The water bottle held up over her head
A relief from all the exam studying
It could be a stress reliever

Water
They say
Is good for everything
A panacea of sorts

She partakes of the water bottle
As her two friends look at each other
They say something
She ignores them

And they walk off
Three of them together
The water bottle girl with her new grasp
And the two happy to be there with her

"THOUGHTS IN THE LIBRARY"

What must they be thinking?
Pouring over books and notes
Are they transported into another world
Suspending their life's experiences
Memories?

Over there
The girl in gray
With long brunette hair
And pretty thin face
Writing with her blue pen with a yellow tip

What is she thinking?
With her pensive
Yet mysterious look
She could be writing a love note
Who could tell?

And her friend
Sitting right next to her
With cropped-up blonde hair
Open purple jacket
Revealing a low cut black shirt

What could she be thinking?
The intensity of the lecture material
The key to life's mystery
That she is about to unlock?
Her pretty face scrunched together

How about this girl right in front?
Probably 24 years old
But looking like she is 18
Sitting with her legs stretched
With a bad posture

Total Depravity

She doesn't look too happy to be here
But I bet she's top of her class
She probably doesn't realize how pretty she is
If she grew her hair a bit more
She could probably be a prom queen

And this one here
With her butt practically slipping off the chair
Bright but tight pink shirt
Manifesting her curves
Even her bra straps that need to be fixed

She does have an interesting hair style
Cropped back in modernesque untidiness
With one thin strand braded
Ending in a blue, heart head-pin
You could tell she's an intense person

She probably puts her heart into everything
From studying to friendships
Housecleaning to well-planned vacations
I wonder how she kisses
She would probably be very intense

It is interesting observing
All the different people who make up
This little space called the library
All the lives that they represent
Collective experiences that would fill the tomes

"THROUGH THE WINDOW"

Through the window
I can see the leaves shaking
Stirred by gentle winds
On a bright sunny day

A big tall tree
With red, purple leaves
Fluttering
Branches moving about

Even short branches join
In a silent spring dance
To conjure up passions
Of the coming summer

From here
The movements are inaudible
Breeze that moves
Cannot be felt

No nature sounds
Hope of spring
Rejuvenation of a new season
Zest for life

In an aquarium for the birds to observe
We sit here
Under the transparent windows
Clear, light-emitting ceiling

Focused on our notes
Many books with small prints
Typing away on our keyboards
Squinting to think

Total Depravity

Feeling a bit of sunshine
Diluted
Penetrating the thick window
Mixed in with artificial lights

Concentrating to squeeze through
A bit of that knowledge
That opens the door to success
Human understanding?

In a fish bowl for the entertainment of the shaking trees
Frolicking about outside
Inside, we remain serious, driven
A sight for the world

Perhaps the trees are shaking
In laughter
Hardly able to contain the joke of life
Hunched humans pouring over texts

Maybe they are moving
In sadness
Watching the wasted youth
And time

It could be that they want to capture
Our attention
To tell us the true meaning of life
What is really important

But we sit here
Ignoring the message of Nature
Working to exist
Existing to work

"TYPING AWAY"

She is typing away
Right behind me
Her fingers caressing the keys
Of her laptop computer
In a gentle motion
I can hardly hear it
But there she is, typing away

I am here
With my back to her
She can see me
I can't see her
But my noise can be heard
My typing is pervading throughout the room
And it's a little pocket computer

The little thing makes noises
As it shakes with each type
What a contrast
As she presses the keys
Making images appear before her big screen
I am squinting just to see what is being typed
This is one tenth the size of hers

I type passionately
Onto my little machine
With a little screen
And negligible memory
And I type with abandon
Not looking to the right or the left
Funny how a little thing can capture me

She must have stopped typing
Because I hear nothing behind me
Maybe she's staring at my head
Thinking that she could find a bald spot

Total Depravity

I type ignoring the silence
Her possible investigation
But I do wonder what was typed on her keyboard

What is being recorded
What is being created
As I tick my keys in fast motion
Digits of my finger rolling onto the board
Ideas come rushing in
And I try to grab them for my little machine
To add to its meager memory

The creation happens
Right before my eyes
In the small machine
That is a part of me
As I unload the thoughts
That has enslaved me
It is a release much needed

I turn around
To see why it's so silent
She's not typing on her big machine
She has grabbed hold of her little phone
Holding it with both her hands
Her face close to it
Pushing the buttons gingerly

She's sending a SMS
A greeting
Perhaps an invitation
She pushes her fingers gingerly against the keys
You could tell she is that kind of a person
Giving attention to detail
Directing her undivided attention to what she cares about

I wonder how she would be
If she were here
Releasing her thoughts

Total Depravity

Onto my portable keyboard
With a tiny screen loosely attached
I bet she would put herself into it
Her ginger attention and intense focus

I am sure she would type as fast
Perhaps faster than I
Stroking the keys with her beautiful fingers
Perhaps she will squint her eyes
I am sure a change would come over her face
Perhaps she will find creative fulfillment
Typing into my little pocket computer

Should I go and ask her?
God forbid
This is a library
And there is protocol
Although she impresses me as a rebel
Waiting to get out
I shan't intrude, at least not now

"UNDER A TREE"

Under a tree she sits
Next to her a heavy bag
In hectic exam time
A space of tranquility and peace

She gazes down her thick book
Perhaps a book on civil liberties
Or a book outlining human anatomy
She sits casually as if there were no exams

The leaves sway slightly back and forth
Fanning her as she enjoys the spring sunshine
Outside in a cozy place
A corner in this big university

She sits musing
Thinking
Reflecting
You could almost see her thoughts run

From inside
She is visible
Through the glass wall
Which affords her no privacy

As if she doesn't even realize
She sits there in her comfort zone
Ignoring the numerous stares thrown in her direction
From inside the building

There she is
Under a tree
Enjoying life
As it should be

"HER BOTTLE OF LIQUID"

She grabs her bottle of liquid
Clasping it with all her fingers
Four fingers extending and enfolding
Meeting her thumb from the other direction
The palm of her hand firmly pressed

Her shiny finger nails reflect light
As her fingers squeeze the bottle
Tighter and tighter
In the silence pervading the room
She doesn't even seem to notice what is around

With a singular purpose
To be satiated
To be moisturized
To be filled
She opens her mouth

Slowly she brings her water bottle
Firmly, almost painfully squeezed
Nearer and nearer to her lips
Ruddy, flushed, glistening
Cap opened, ready to do her bid

With nonchalant determination
She lifts up the bottle
Revealing its source of succor
And she drinks what's inside
Her lips enclosing the opening

Her muscles move
Her neck shows
Her lips tighter
As liquid flows into her being
Rejuvenating her, filling her up

"IMAGES"

Pages open
Chewing on the nails
Raised eye brows
Searching for something
Not in the pages of the thick book
Knowledge it might contain
Benefits it does hold
Intellectually, that is
The quest is of another sort
Dreams of rolling hills
Gentle streams flowing
Cloth laid spread
For a heavenly picnic
Biting of an apple
Teeth sinking deeply in
Chewing of a ham sandwich
With two slices of Swiss cheese
Whipped cream laden strawberry tart
Mixed in with bubbly champagne
The sight of the blast still in the air

"BASE PASSIONS"

It is an effusion of emotions
Unsubstantiated and irrational
Desire to enwrap, enfold
Cover with all of one's being

No purpose
No intention
No plans
Nothing beyond instant gratification

To capture the moment
Without even exchange of names
Understanding of who she is
Making myself known to her

Connecting at the simplest human level
Perhaps the most honest of connections
Without white lies
With no pretensions

Two bodies laid bare
Just as
To enjoy what there is
What is seen

Only the grunting of human desires
Longing followed by longing
Effusion of human essence intermingled in each other
Fear mixed with happiness

Self-abandon
Giving of self
Exchange of all that one can see
And feel

Total Depravity

A one time meeting
With no follow up
Continuation
A moment frozen in time

Base desires
Raging
Agreed
Satisfied

"DETERRENCE"

The sheer knowledge
That she belongs to another
Happily and willingly
Is deterrence enough

Her sitting together with him
In close proximity
Playfully caressing
The inside of his upper thigh

Walking hand in hand
Smiling
Joking
Playful

Obviously she is happy
Perhaps she is enjoying
The happiest moments of her life
Who am I to mettle with that?

What do I want from her?
It is pure, unadulterated desire
Wanting her body
Desiring her just for her naked beauty

Wanting pleasure
To pleasure her
And to be pleasured by her
It is an animal desire

Filled with desire to engage in acts
That you could never tell anyone about
Because of its very raw nature
Difficult even to utter aloud even to myself

Total Depravity

But oh, what could be done
I would bring her to the seventh heaven
Of pleasure and ecstasy
Something she could only have imagined

But she is happy
Obviously content in her relationship
And life
In sweet coupleness

I desire her
To feel her
To press against her
To lick her all over

But that would not be right
I cannot give her pleasure
As great as it might be
And break up her life

It is a kind of deterrent
A cosmic force of ethics
The knowledge of the possibility
Of a living being's life interrupted

A greater deterrent than
Mere circumstances
Boundaries created geographically
Physically and mentally

It is a cosmic deterrent
That forces one not to act
However much temporary pleasure
I might be able to present to her

The fact remains
I want her just for her body
I don't want a relationship
Or to have her in a meaningful relationship

Total Depravity

It is a base passion
That strikes men out of the blue
And women too
I suppose

If she were unhappy
I could reason
I will bring her a moment's pleasure
To brighten up her day

Pleasure for her to treasure
For the rest of her life
Sensations to feel in her times of sadness
Memories to keep her little fire burning

But all my human rationale
To justify my physical desire
Wish to gratify her every sexual need
Fails

She is happy in her relationship
Her life may be complete with him
And I can't break up her joy attached to life
It would be like murdering someone

If she were alone
Did not care about anyone so happily
In a state of adventure
Or just like the rest of us

I would imagine
More would be possible
Perhaps
If she wanted

But I am presented with deterrence
A type of Natural Law
Perhaps imposed on me by God
To keep me away from a certain fornication

"DRAWN"

I don't know why
But I am drawn

It might be her sheer beauty
For there is no beauty like hers

It could be her pleasant ways
She is agreeable beyond measure

Perhaps it's her kind heart
Her gentle spirit shows her inner beauty

I do like her smiles
They brighten the whole world

Or her clear, beautiful eyes
They reach out to my soul

How she walks
I could see myself walking in sync

The way she sings
Almost as beautiful as she looks

Her movements
There is grace in each motion

Her voice melts
Like a warm fire in a mountain cabin

I think about her
And her glorious ways

Soft gentleness mixed with
Brutal, merciless beauty

Total Depravity

I wonder if she is drawn
The way I am

"I MET HER"

She was there
The coy beauty
With subtle sensuality
Who only raised
The basest of my passions

It turned out she knew
Some people that I have met before
In sacred contexts
Should I have felt guilty
For all my thoughts of her sensual body?

Her smooth, toned stomach
Revealed as she stretched between readings
Her thin bare arms without blemish
That would feel soft to my touch

Her ruddy, pouty lips
Ready to be kissed and sucked
Her mysterious eyes
That betray her apparent innocence

Her non-blonde hair
Enticing in ways that would surprise any soul
Her white neck
Stretched out to be devoured

And the beauty of her youth
Embodied in her firm, curvaceous breasts
Her body moves in ways
That races your heart beat

I saw her again
In her sensual package
And I could not contain
My animal desires

Total Depravity

I could not think of sweet
Romanic things, like flowers
I could only imagine
How she would look

I only wanted to unpackage
Her body's own flower
To stroke and to taste
To feel with the tip of my tongue

I could not think of holding her hand
Like sweet boyfriends do
But to squeeze her naked body tightly
Bringing her whole womanhood into my male essence

I could not think about stroking her hair
With the gentleness of a caring one
But rather to hold her hair and head tight
As I entered her enticing body over and over again

I could not think of holding her gently by her waist
But rather wanted to squeeze her butt until she would go blue
And bite her sumptuous breasts
Until she would cry in pleasure

She sat there against the wall
Looking blankly into space
And I couldn't resist
But to find out who she was

Should I feel guilty for the way I feel?
Wanting to engage her purely on a physical level
Overriding passions clouding perspicuity of thought
Desiring her for her body

We have mutual friends
In a sacred space no less
But I cannot say that I could resist or care
If she allowed me to pleasure her

"PASSING BY"

It was a split second
That divided two worlds
Me on this side
And her on the other side

As she passed by
On her bicycle
I saw flashes of images
Flood of memories

I let out a grunt in response
But nothing tangible
Perhaps not audible to her
In a split second, she was gone

In a moment of time
When one sees life flashing by
A moment that could open doors
Or keep the doors closed and locked

It was hard to find the key
The right key
That would unlock the lock
The key that I had did not work

What can I do?
But see the bicycle
And the special rider on it
Go in the other direction

As I stood there
Not knowing how to bring it back
The second that just passed
The bicycle that has left the scene

Total Depravity

Time passed mercilessly
Cars passed by insensitively
Those walking kept walking
I could not but pick up my steps

And walk I did
For my appointment
To help others
Forgetting about my personal needs

"PURPLE"

The landscape is colored in purple
Visibly scattered across the surface
As if to send a message
Perhaps of friendship

Different shades of purple
Dark purple
Light purple
In-between purple

Purple shirts
Varying textures
Worn
Brightening up the room

The message?
It is friendship
It was friendship
It will only be friendship

Who knows?
Who can tell?
What the message is
The color purple

Sitting there
At a distance
The blonde with the purple shirt
Smiles and whispers inaudibly

Flipping the pages
The one with her back turned
Black hair falling on her shoulders
She seems quite engaged

And the one right in front of me

Total Depravity

With the light shade of purple
Brunette with blonde highlights
Holds her book against her chest

Like a new born babe
Who needs delicate attention
Her delicate ruddy fingers
Gently resting on the white pages

Her lips kissing the tip
Of the ballpoint pen
Her well-groomed hair
Resting deliberately on her neck

With her every movement
She reveals her playful side
Even a hint of smile
Playing on her red lips

The color purple
Perhaps that of friendship
Conjures not in her body
Thoughts of friendship

As her shirt sticks temptingly
Onto her skin
Outlining her every form
Her every curve

Revealing
Indicating
What is underneath
Curvaceous female form

Not made for friendship
Of platonic kind
Her milky skin
Blends into the purple shirt

Total Depravity

Her woman's curves
Beckoning a man's touch
As she moves
And presses her arm

Against her breasts
Accentuating new curves
Rolling hills of Armageddon
At least the fiery passions thereof

A friend in green walks over
Engages her in conversation
In practiced innocence
She moves and smiles

With a genuine sensuality
She probably is yet discovering
And she moves
Her body in expressive ways

As if in a club
Somewhat out of place
In the library
But a natural flow of movement

On her
Purple cannot denote a color
Other than sensual invitation
The kind a boy longs for

What I would do to her purple shirt
I cannot even say
But I know that whatever it is
It would involve an element of pleasure

There are a million ways
A billion things
That I would love to do
And it's not just a rudely awoken passion speaking

Total Depravity

For her ways
With her subtle sensuality
Couched sexual passion
Subdued raw beauty

They do create
Creativity upon creativity
In the ways of a man
To a woman

They are not delicate desires
Which are shaken to realization
It is an animal instinct
To satiate and to be satiated by

To extend
To draw close
To touch
To press

It is a good thing
Perhaps good is not the word
That this is a library
An austere prison against such things

Were this a setting
Remotely resembling a place
Of fraternization
Social intercourse

Who knows what would happen?
Certainly not a platonic friendship
Her purple shirt clad feminine form
Paints all in black and white

It would be all or nothing
Pleasure or pain
Ecstasy or numbness
Sensual cry or total silence

Total Depravity

It is the form
The combination
Of innocence and rawness
Such as hers

That have moved nations
Destroyed peoples
Made a man great
Passions for the books

She is there
Writing away
Studying for her exams
Looking intently into her work

And I can think only about
How she would look
Exerting her intense energy
In a passionate embrace

Her form laid bare
In an enthusiastic entanglement
Breaking social barriers
And entering into freedom

Restraints stripped away
Guards down
Raw creativity engaged
In every possible way

And she writes and writes
I cannot think but to imagine
How she would be
How she would sound

It is the fact of the library
That rescues
Or condemns
One in such a situation

Total Depravity

Her purpleness
Is more passionate than the red
On her lips
Like a rose unplucked from the field

On a sunny day
Underneath the bright sunshine
With slight breeze caressing the body
Leaves falling sensuously

In her purpleness she remains
Now her book pressed tightly against her succulent breasts
As she takes a short break
From her intense activity

I think I will change my attitude toward purple
There are moments that come
When past categories are destroyed
And a new meaning arises

She now writes
Her book pressed against her curves
Her cheeks flushed red
Her delicate hands beautiful as ever

And I remain
Admiring in silence
From this prisoner cell of a library
Where silence is the law

But I cannot help
But to wonder
Who she is
What she would be like

I discover a little bit of myself
In the purple field
Confronted by the subtle purple
With a thrust of burning fire within

"SHE RAISES HER FINGER"

She raises her finger
And brushes her hair
Long and blonde
With a single, decisive stroke

She writes
As her golden hair rests
Streaming down her long bare arms
Strands falling enticingly on her breasts

It's like a jungle
Passionate and jubilant
Mysterious and dangerous
A serene place of rest

A place where I could rest my head
With no worries in the world
Hearing the constant soft breathing of nature
Feeling the rise and fall of soft leaves

I would love to run my toes
Underneath the fallen leaves
Tapping gently and softly
Feeling the texture of the dust-formed matter

Toes sinking under the sand in a tropical white beach
So would my toes sink down the soft surface
Reshaping every curve
Pressing every one of nature's buttons

She raises her finger
Lifts a bunch of her frizzy blonde hair
Lets them fall, cascading down
Free fall, flying down

Total Depravity

Like the powerful drop of Niagara Falls
They draw my eyes in their singular motion
Falling and falling
Hitting her uncovered shoulders

The jungle beckons
In the heat of early summer
To be discovered
To be uncovered

Greenness of the jungle
So innocent, yet so passionate
Who knows what the nature's key might open?
What I will experience?

Life?
Death?
Life and death intertwined?
Ethereal ecstasy of another world?

Beyond death
Beyond life
The jungle remains but a black hole
Drawing me, pulling me closer and closer

"THE SMILE"

It is a smile frozen in time
Like a picture out of my photo album
Clear as day
Certainly not doing justice to reality

What lies behind the smile
I do not know
Nor does she
Least of all

In the mystery of life
With puzzles
Created and compounded daily
With no real solution

Maze that seems endless
With walls higher than the heavens
Little light to guide
With pitfalls everywhere

The smile betrays
Mesmerizes
Hypnotizes
Misleads

She doesn't know
Nor do I
What lies beyond the smile
Nor do I care

Whatever slings and arrows of outrageous fortune
I would embrace them all
To have that smile
For her to abandon that smile to me willingly

"THE WAY SHE MOVED"

It was on a floor
Filled with music come alive
Bodies moving
In a regular pattern

But there she was
The way she moved
Stuck out like a sore thumb
She was different

She undulated her torso
And through the shirt slightly raised
Her stomach muscles moved like gentle waters
Smooth white surface undisturbed

And her arms gently caressed her sides
As her head moved slightly from side to side
Her beautiful eyes shining like the moon
Her legs firm but limber

She moved in a belly dance
Fit for the kings
Enticing every eye
Which came within 10 feet of her

She moved
In beautiful subtlety
As beats pulsated
Shaking the room

Her bare arms
Pointed to her naked stomach
And the promise that it offered
Temptation that it forced

Total Depravity

There in the midst of male desires
We danced
Appreciating
The beauty of the form

She moved
And the world around her moved with her
Her smile showed that she understood
After all, she was a gift from heaven

"DAMPENED LAWN"

Sitting there
On top of prickly grass
Dampened by summer moistures
I can feel the permeation
Of that which is a part of nature

I sit, thinking about the beauty of the skies
Vast without end
As I feel the soft, flat surface
Underneath me
Tickling me

I feel the heat of the sun
Slowly raising my body temperature
And drops of sweat gathering on my neck
As I feel the coolness of the wet grass
Perhaps it is the cold sweat of the earth

I can feel the soft texture of the grass below me
As I gather myself in reflection
About the moment
And the pleasure that I feel
That is encapsulated in time

I know that it is here
With a firm ground below me
My body pressing against the earth
Its beautiful form
That I have found a moment of heaven on earth

I feel the breeze passing by
Cooling my sun-pressed being
And I still feel the fire within
Kindled by the intensity of sun's embrace

Total Depravity

And I sit in a type of ecstatic release

Enjoying the atmosphere and its temptations
The lubricated mound pushing against me
The heat of spring passions
The cooling of liquids on my body
The simple pleasure of nature that is there to enjoy

"GRASS AND WHITE FLOWERS"

Walking along the road
Familiar
Beautiful
Brightened by spring sunshine
In the warmth
A foretaste of summer
I walk
Eagerly towards
The nice patch of grass
Just in front of the Fire Station
Ready to extinguish any burning fire
Next to the Police Station
Adding to the element of danger
I walk knowing
That at any moment
A siren could be heard
Breaking the idyllic silence
A calm spring morning
And I walk
Lightly as I could on the grass
Gently massaging the natural stubs
Under my feet
As the audible sound of the contact
Between me and the earth's beauty
Rises in regular beat
And I could almost feel the moisture
That naturally fills the earth's body
And smell the freshness of spring's maiden call
I notice the beauty of white flowers
Having sprung up all over the field
As if over night
Perhaps I only began to notice
They were just always there
And I see the beauty in individuality
The unique pulchritude of each and every white flower
That is dotting the landscape

Total Depravity

Presenting an orgy of pleasure for the senses
And the nature's delight that is distinctive
But a part of the common experience
The property of each and every one
Each white flower radiant
Suggestive of the mystery of nature
Of which they are all a part
And in which they delight
Underneath the blue skies
In the warmth of fresh Spring morn
In the vast landscape
Collectively enhancing the allure
Of the moist, life-giving grass patch

"MOTIONLESS"

Motionless
Surely it is
As I glance haphazardly out the window
Ceiling transparent as the sky
The clouds seem to stand still
Having come to a halt
Halt!

Then, I look
Motionless
Looking intently at a large cloud mass
And notice
It is not still
It is not standing
It is not frozen
It is alive

Slowly moving
From here to there
The white cloud moves
And the rest follow
Making a path on the blue sky
Vast and endless
Enticing my eyes to follow
The beautiful gentle movement

Motionless
It is not
Neither do I feel
Motionless
As my eyes follow
The celestial movement
Of a soft white cloud
Making its advance in the vast sky

"THE GLACIER"

Spreading down the mountain
On a summer day
As if forgetting that the winter has gone
Remains solid
Firm
The icy beauty
Lying with her back against the earth
Her smooth belly facing towards the sky
Connecting the mystery of heaven
With the life-filled earth
Often
Snow glides down this body
In a gentle roll
White
Brightly deflecting the summer sun
A wonder of nature
So beautiful to behold
Eyes always reluctant to depart
From the natural beauty
Somehow formed
Matter arranged to create a beautiful whole
All holding together like the beauty of perfection
I could see one walking on the edge
Another trying to climb
From a distance
I see the futile efforts of beginners
So unaccustomed to the slippery surface
I think to myself
How I might traverse the unwritten paths of the
Beautiful glacier
So much more beautiful in the summer time
When its beautiful body stands out
Against the backdrop of all that is summer
Opposite of summer
Yet a part of it
Virginal in her pure appearance

Total Depravity

Passionate in the strength of the cold
Fiery in her potential to satisfy
Withstanding the summer season
In the middle of all that has changed
She lies firmly against the ground
With her face facing towards the sky
Looking at endless possibilities that are out there
Cold
Yet open
Frozen
But welcoming
I don't know if my summer shoes will be able to hold
And if I would be able to go on top of the beautiful form
Or if I will slide down
Go up
Slide down again
Go up again
Up and down
In an effort to reach the crown of her beauty
The climax of natural development
And claim her as my own
I anticipate the climb
Of the beautiful summer glacier

"THE OASIS"

Thin white line marks the path to paradise
In the vast expanse of soft, undulating sandy desert
First, I traverse the narrow path with my eyes
Slowly outlining the highlighted line
I could almost see my glance making its imprint
In the enticing desert
Curves toned by years of gently stroking wind
Contours gliding, smooth like purple satin sheets
Holding wonders of mystery
Endless supply of oh-so-very-touchable sand
Finer than the sand of Venice Beach
Supporting the thong-clad bottoms of youth
It seems even the sand has become tan
In the warmth of sunshine
Were sunshine a boy and the vast desert a girl
They would not part
United like one body
Conjoined at each end
In the flowing tanned body of sand
The white road leads to the oasis
Down yonder
Deep inside
Hidden away
Covered by the flowing leaves of palm trees
Water sprouting from within
Warm
Very liquid
Energizing in a particular way
The path starts on the smooth surface
Back yonder
Over the shoulder of that hill
Rising above
Facing the heaven
The white path leads toward a mound
Glorious and well-formed
Remaining erect in the space of warmth

Total Depravity

An enjoyable path it is
I know it is a road filled with pleasure
As my toes presses against the surface
Sand sinking between my toes
Feeling the definite texture of its being
My foot would massage the path
Each step taken with tenderness
I would think of the juicy waters of the oasis
Then, I would reach over with both hands
Cupped, ready to partake
I will plunge my fingers deep inside
Feeling the warmth of sun-soaked fluids
But I know that my hands will not only touch
The warm source of life
I would lap up the juices with my tongue
Like a dog deprived of water in summer heat
I would lick with a passion intense
Excitement rising to a crescendo
Until the whole being shutters with ecstasy
My lips gently touching the surface
While my tongue makes the seeking plunge
The path of pleasure
United like one body
Pressed gently in a firm embrace
White path traversed
Yet, printed all over with my being
Oh, how the desert surface would move!
The surface tingly from sensation
Sensitive to the slightest stroke of gentle wind
The palm trees will shake side to side
As the sweet aroma rises
And I become one
My lips in the wet lips of the oasis
Palm leaves shaking in pleasure
Shrieking, expressing pleasure in its own way
Gently towards that oasis I amble
No need to hurry there
There is all the time in the world

Total Depravity

I take every step with pleasure
Wanting to make drinking from the oasis
That much more pleasurable
For hours I would follow the white path
Enticing tanned body of delicate sand
Might provide me with diversion
Certainly not in vain
For being lost in this desert body
Will certainly add to the pleasure
When my tongue touches the wet oasis

"BEYOND"

Her reddish brown hair
Is spread on her chest
As she tilts her head
Looking out the window

Against her black sweater
Her hair sits in contrast
Atop her perky breasts
In the stilted flatness of the library

Her eyes piercing their blueness
Out the window
Scene of white murkiness
Ready to be poured down upon by looming rain

Her clear white skin
Covered by the weight of dark law books
Gravity versus clarity
Translucence contrasting complexity

She looks beyond
Past the window
Transcending the objects outside
To a point beyond visible reality

Her head is slightly bowed
As if recognizing a reality beyond reality
Her massive hair reaching far and wide
Like the aspirations that lie beyond those blue eyes

"CLICK, SLIP, FLIP"

Click, click, click
Computer keys are pressed
By individuals somewhere in the library

Computing
Imputing
Perhaps surfing the web

Slick, slick, slick
The green highlighter glides across the page
Of some European Union law textbook

Flip, flip, flip
Pages with copious notes turn
Aggressively in frustration

Slick, flip, slip
Flip, slick, flip
Click, click, click

Sounds seem intensified
In the silence
Absent of human voices

Outside the library
There are trees
Naked, without any leaves

Click, slick, flip
Unfriendly sounds blend in the bleak background
As eager faces learn their a-b-c's

"THROUGH THE GARDEN"

Through the Garden
I walk
Treading the well-groomed grass
Beautiful flowers outlining the pathways

It's a bed where flowers lie
With their bright faces pointed skyward
With their long necks stretched back
And their leaves fluttering about

As the gentle breeze comes over them
Like the gentle stroke of a soft hand
Over the smooth surface of satin sheets
Blowing nature's sweet kisses

Gathered together for colluding to do something mysterious
They sit together
Huddled together
Half lying in their stretched form

As in symposia
Or in a mystery rite
Being initiated into the wonders of the world
And their secrets

They are gathered
In all their glory
Huddled together
In sumptuous groupings

There they are
In the garden
Beautiful and delicate
Strong and gentle

Total Depravity

Emitting beauty
And what wonders their scent portends
All that could be beyond the surface
What is deep inside

I walk through the Garden
Drunk in the beauty of the situation
Not knowing what to do or how to act
Paralyzed by the arrow fired by Nature's strongest bow

I walk through the garden
Flowers gently protecting the surface
Beauty betraying the power
The force of the nature's garden

"THE SUN RISES"

The sun rises in a new dawn
Morning filled with anticipation
A new year's morning
The day completely open

What will be will be
The Sages have said
Over and over again
Resignation?

Like that morning on First Easter
There is the initial disappointment
At the empty tomb
Who knows what happened?

But that initial disappointment left behind
Exultation followed
At the angel's announcement
He is risen!

Seeming emptiness
Actual fulfillment
Apparent tragedy
Miraculous reality

The sun rises
Pushing back darkness
Expelling evil
Bringing in what is good

It will be a good day
A new world order
When all is made new
In the power of the resurrection

Printed in the United States
19891LVS00007B/300